致老师和家长们

·

《儿童汉语》是为学龄前的外国儿童学习汉语用的初级读本。

本套教材分为三册,每册二十课。第一册以语音为主,反复进行四声的基本功训练。第二、三册主要介绍汉语的一些基本句式,浅显易懂。每册后附辅导材料。

本套教材突出实用的原则,从儿童日常生活中最熟悉的事物入手,教给他们生活中使用最多的一些词汇,学会说一些简单的生活用语。

本套教材体现了较强的趣味性,选取儿童感兴趣的话题,反映儿童自己的生活,主人公是中国和外国的孩子,从内容上体现儿童的特点,如课文中有游戏、小孩"过家家"、小兔、小狗、孙悟空、做梦到月亮上去旅行等。

本套教材全部采用对话形式,并适当穿插一些谜语、儿歌、游戏、画画等,形式活泼引人,语言生动,图文并茂。

学完这三册书后,能掌握一些最基本的语言材料,为将来系统地、正规地学习汉语打下基础。

为了使您的孩子能准确地掌握发音,我们为本套教材配备了标准录音磁带。

编　者

一九八六年二月

To Teachers and Parents

Chinese for Children is an elementary textbook designed especially for the teaching of Chinese to children abroad of pre-school age.

There are three volumes in all, each consisting of twenty lessons. Volume I is aimed at teaching children Chinese pronunciation and the four tones by means of plenty of pronunciation drills; volumes II and III deal mainly with basic sentence patterns which are simple and easily understood by children. Each volume includes an appendix of teacher's notes.

This set of books takes a practical approach, presenting the children with words and phrases most useful in their every day life.

The topics chosen for each text are interesting to children because they focus on a child's world: it is children, Chinese and foreign, who speak in the text, and talk about children's games such as playing doctor, and tell stories such as the Monkey King and even of a journey to the moon in their dreams.

The texts are in the form of dialogue, enlivened with riddles, nursery rhymes, games and drawings. Its colourful language, together with a large number of illustrations, make this book most appealing to children.

After completing this set of books, children will have a basic knowledge of the Chinese language: pronunciation, a 340-character vocabulary, and some basic sentence patterns, thus laying a solid foundation for future study of the Chinese language.

To help your children pronounce Chinese correctly, we have also produced the cassette tapes to accompany the texts.

The Compilers.
February, 1986

Contents

1 　　叔叔请进

请 to ask qǐng	坐 to sit zuò	上班 to go to work shàngbān
进 to enter jìn	谢谢 to thank xièxie	商店 shop shāngdiàn
您 you nín	家 home, family jiā	

叔叔请进!　Shūshu qǐng jìn!
　Uncle, please come in!

请坐!　Qǐng zuò!
　Please sit down!

谢谢。你爸爸在家吗?　Xièxie. Nǐ bàba zài jiā ma?
Thank you. Is your father in?

爸爸不在家。　Bàba bú zài jiā.
　No, he isn't.

他去哪儿了?　Tā qù nǎr le?
Where has he gone?

爸爸上班了。　Bàba shàng bān le.
　He has gone to work.

妈妈呢?　Māma ne?
What about your mother?

妈妈去商店了。　Māma qù shāngdiàn le.
Mother has gone to the shop.

阿姨好！

你好！你在做什么呢？

我玩儿呢。

你妈妈在家吗？

妈妈不在家。

她去哪儿了？

她去学校了。

你爸爸呢？

爸爸在家,阿姨请进！

LOOK.   SAY.   WRITE

老师_____！

冬冬去哪儿了？   芳子去哪儿了？

3

2   小小运动会

运动会 sports meet
yùndònghuì

昨天 yesterday
zuótiān

开（会）to have(a meeting)
kāi (huì)

跳高 high jump
tiàogāo

赛跑 to run a race
sàipǎo

跑 to run
pǎo

跳 to jump
tiào

高 high
gāo

4

爸爸,昨天我们开运动会了。
Dad, we had a sports meet yesterday.

Bàba, zuótiān wǒmen kāi yùndònghuì le.

你跳高了吗?
Did you take part in high jump?

Nǐ tiàogāo le ma?

我没(有)跳高,
No, I didn't.

Wǒ méi (you) tiàogāo,

我赛跑了。
I ran a race.

wǒ sàipǎo le.

谁跑得最快?
Who ran the fastest?

Shuí pǎode zuì kuài?

冬冬跑得最快。
Dongdong ran the fastest.

Dōngdong pǎode zuì kuài.

谁跳得最高?
Who jumped the highest?

Shuí tiàode zuì gāo?

兰兰跳得最高。
Lanlan jumped the highest.

Lánlan tiàode zuì gāo.

READ ALOUD

他们在做什么呢？

　　他们在开运动会呢。

谁跑得最快？

　　兔子跑得最快。

谁跳得最远（yuǎn far）？

　　青蛙（qīngwā frog）跳得最远。

谁跳得最高？

　　蚱蜢（zhàměng grasshopper）跳得最高。

LOOK.　SAY.　WRITE

昨天你们做什么了？

昨天你去学校了吗？

3 打电话

打（电话） to make (a telephone call), dǎ (diànhuà)

喂 wèi hello (on the telephone)

呀 ya

忙 máng busy

电话 diànhuà telephone

明天 míngtiān tomorrow

能 néng can

见 jiàn to see

喂，谁呀？
Hello, who is it, please?

Wèi, shuí ya?

我是芳子。
This is Fangzi speaking.

Wǒ shì Fāngzǐ.

你是玛丽吗？
Is that Mary speaking?

Nǐ shì Mǎlì ma?

我是玛丽。
Yes，it is.

Wǒ shì Mǎlì.

你好，玛丽。
Hello, Mary．

Nǐ hǎo, Mǎlì.

你忙不忙？
Are you busy?

Nǐ máng bù máng?

我不忙。
I'm not busy.

Wǒ bù máng.

明天是我的生日。
It's my birthday tomorrow.

Míngtiān shì wǒde shēngri.

你能不能来我家？
Can you come to my house?

Nǐ néng bù néng lái wǒ jiā?

能。
Yes, I can.

Néng.

好，明天见。
O.K. See you tomorrow.

Hǎo, míngtiān jiàn.

明天见。
See you tomorrow.

Míngtiān jiàn.

喂？

您好，阿姨。兰兰在家吗？

兰兰不在家，你是谁呀？

我是冬冬。阿姨，兰兰去哪儿了？

她去天安门了。

她今天去不去学校？

今天是星期日，她不去学校。

您能不能告诉（gàosu　tell）她，

明天八点半开运动会。

好，谢谢你。

不谢。阿姨再见。

再见。

LOOK.　SAY.　WRITE

_____？
（写不写）

_____？
（穿不穿）

_____？
（要不要）

_____？
（有没有）

4 一件礼物

礼物 present
lǐwù

蛋糕 cake
dàngāo

听 to listen
tīng

祝 to wish, to congratulate
zhù

送 to give (a present)
sòng

猜 to guess
cāi

糖 sweets, candy
táng

金鱼 gold fish
jīnyú

大 big
dà

听, 冬冬来了。   Tīng, Dōngdong láile.
Listen, here comes Dongdong.

芳子, 祝你生日好!   Fāngzǐ, zhù nǐ shēngri hǎo!
Happy birthday, Fangzi!

谢谢。   Xièxie.
Thank you.

我送你一件礼物。   Wǒ sòng nǐ yí jiàn lǐwù.
Here is a present from me.

什么礼物?   Shénme lǐwù?
What is it?

你猜。   Nǐ cāi.
Have a guess

是大蛋糕。对不对?   Shì dàdàngāo. Duì bu duì?
It's a big cake. Right?

不对。   Bú duì.
No.

是糖?   Shì táng?
Candies?

也不对。   Yě bú duì.
Wrong again.

你看, 这是什么?   Nǐ kàn, zhè shì shénme?
Look, what is it?

小金鱼!   Xiǎojīnyú!
Little gold fish!

READ ALOUD

今天是妈妈的生日，爸爸、哥哥（gēge）、妹妹（mèimei）都给（gěi）妈妈一件礼物。爸爸送妈妈一件毛衣，哥哥送妈妈一个生日蛋糕，妹妹送妈妈一盒（hé box）糖。小红给妈妈什么呢？她画了一张画儿，上边有很多花儿，还写了六个字："祝妈妈生日好！"

LOOK. SAY. WRITE

他送阿姨什么？

_____。

谁送玛丽一只小鸟？

_____。

奶奶给她什么？

_____。

芳子教谁《儿童汉语》？

_____。

5   讲故事

讲 to tell jiǎng	给 for, to gěi	过 *aspectual particle* guò
故事 story gùshi	以前 ago, before yǐqián	乌龟 tortoise wūguī
爷爷 grandpa, granddad yéye	电影 film diànyǐngr	孙悟空 the Monkey King Sūn Wùkōng

老爷爷，您给我们讲个故事，好吗？
Grandpa, please tell us a story.

Lǎoyéye, nín gěi wǒmen jiǎng ge gùshi, hǎo ma?

好。很早很早以前，
All right. Once upon a time,

Hǎo. Hěn zǎo hěn zǎo yǐqián,

有一只小兔和一只小乌龟……
there was a hare and a tortoise...

yǒu yì zhī xiǎotù hé yì zhī xiǎowūguī ......

这个故事我们听过了。
We have heard the story.

Zhège gùshi wǒmen tīngguo le.

很早很早以前，
Once upon a time,

Hěn zǎo hěn zǎo yǐqián,

有一只小羊……
there was a little lamb...

yǒu yì zhī xiǎoyáng ......

这个，我们也看过电影了。
We have seen this film, too.

Zhège, wǒmen yě kànguo diànyǐngr le.

你们喜欢听什么呢？
What do you like listening to?

Nǐmen xǐhuan tīng shénme ne?

我们最喜欢听孙悟空的故事。
We like to listen to the story of the Monkey King best.

Wǒmen zuì xǐhuān tīng Sūn Wùkōng de gùshi.

老师好！老师，您给我们讲一个故事吧。

你们喜欢听什么故事呢？

我喜欢听小白兔的故事。

不好，不好。我要听孙悟空的故事。

孙悟空的故事老师讲过了。

我给你们讲"渔夫（yú fū　fisherman）和金鱼"的故事吧。

LOOK.　SAY.　WRITE

芳子去过天安门吗？

＿＿＿＿＿＿＿。

你学过这个汉字吗？

＿＿＿＿＿＿＿。

谁在给娃娃穿衣服呢？

＿＿＿＿＿＿＿。

冬冬在给谁打电话呢？

＿＿＿＿＿＿＿。

6 北海公园

北海公园 Beihai Park
Běihǎi Gōngyuán

山 hill
shān

还 as well
hái

湖 lake
hú

划 to row
huá

跟 with
gēn

船 boat, ship
chuán

爬 to climb
pá

一起 together
yìqǐ

玛丽,你去过北海公园吗?

Have you ever been
to Beihai Park, Mary?

Mǎlì, nǐ qùguo Běihǎi
Gōngyuán ma?

没有去过。

No, I haven't.

Méiyou qùguo.

北海公园里有山吗?

Is there a hill in Beihai Park?

Běihǎi Gōngyuán
li yǒu shān ma?

有山,还有湖。

Yes, and there is a lake as well.

Yǒu shān, háiyǒu hú.

在那儿能划船吗?

Can people go rowing there?

Zài nàr néng huá
chuán ma?

能,我在那儿划过船,

Yes. I've been rowing there,

Néng, wǒ zài nàr
huáguò chuán,

还爬过山。

and I've climbed the hill, too.

hái páguo shān.

星期天你跟我们一起去,好吗?

Will you go with us on Sunday?

Xīngqītiān nǐ gēn wǒmen
yìqǐ qù, hǎo ma?

好。

Certainly.

Hǎo.

READ ALOUD

　　北京有一个很大的公园，叫北海公园。公园里有山，有湖，山上还有一个白塔(tǎ　　pagoda)。那儿的树和花儿真多，小鸟 在树上唱歌，蝴蝶(húdié　　butterfly)在花儿里跳舞。

　　冬冬最喜欢北海公园。星期天，他跟爸爸、妈妈在公园里划船。冬冬划船划得很好，爬山也爬得很快，他们玩得真高兴(gāo xìng　　happy)。

LOOK.　SAY.　WRITE

他在哪儿游泳？

他在＿＿＿＿里游泳。

他们在哪儿听故事？

他们在＿＿＿＿里听故事。

她跟谁一起滑冰？

她跟＿＿＿＿一起滑冰。

他跟谁一起看电影？

他跟＿＿＿＿一起看电影。

7　坐电车

电车　tram diànchē	张 *measure word* zhāng	车　vehicle chē
买　to buy mǎi	到　to go to, 　　to arrive dào	要　will, 　　to be going to yào
票　ticket piào	吧 *modal particle* ba	下　to get off xià

请买票。
    Fares, please.

    阿姨,买三张(票)。
    Auntie, three tickets, please.

到哪儿?
    Where to?

    北海公园。
    Beihai Park.

    老爷爷,您坐这儿吧。
    Grandpa, please sit here.

好孩子,谢谢你们。
    You're good children,
    thank you.

不谢。
    Not at all.

    ……

    北海要到了,
    We're almost at Beihai.

    老爷爷,我们要下车了。
    Grandpa, we're going to get off.

    再见。
    Good-bye.

再见。
Bye-bye.

Qǐng mǎi piào.

    Āyí,mǎi sān zhāng
    (piào).

Dào nǎr?

    Běihǎi Gōngyuán.

    Lǎoyéye, nín zuò zhèr
    ba.

Hǎo háizi, xièxie nǐmen.

    Bú xiè.

    ……

    Běihǎi yào dàole,

    lǎoyéye, wǒmen yào
    xià chē le.

    Zàijiàn.

Zàijiàn.

阿姨,去动物园（dòngwùyuán the zoo）坐几路（jǐlù
which number）车？

坐103路电车。

谢谢您。

不谢。

叔叔,买票。

到哪儿？

到动物园。

买几张？

两张。

LOOK.　SAY.　WRITE

车还没有来吗？

车＿＿＿＿＿了。

北海到了。

快,我们要＿＿＿＿＿了。

快跑!

要＿＿＿＿＿了。

今天真冷。

要＿＿＿＿＿了。

8   去海边

海边 seaside
hǎibiānr

放（假） to have
(a holiday)
fàng (jià)

暑假 summer hohidays,
summer vacation
shǔjià

旅行 to travel
lǚxíng

哥哥 (elder) brother
gēge

怎么 how
zěnme

火车 train
huǒchē

第 *ordinal prefix*
(-st, -nd, -rd)
dì

次 time
cì

快要放暑假了。
Summer holidays will begin very soon.

Kuài yào fàng shǔjià le.

暑假你去哪儿旅行？
Where are you going to go during the holidays?

Shǔjià nǐ qù nǎr lǚxíng?

我去海边旅行。
I'm going to the seaside.

Wǒ qù hǎibiānr lǚxíng.

你跟谁一起去？
Whom are you going to go with?

Nǐ gēn shuí yìqǐ qù?

我跟爸爸、妈妈、哥哥一起去。
With my father, mother and brother.

Wǒ gēn bàba, māma, gēge yìqǐ qù.

你们怎么去？
How are you going to go there?

Nǐmen zěnme qù?

我们坐火车去。
By train.

Wǒmen zuò huǒchē qù.

你以前去过海边吗？
Have you ever been to the seaside?

Nǐ yǐqián qùguo hǎibiānr ma?

没有，这是第一次。
No. This is the first time.

Méiyou, zhè shì dì yī cì.

祝你玩得好。
Have a good time.

Zhù nǐ wánrde hǎo.

READ ALOUD

寒假(hánjià，winter holiday， winter vacation)到了，玛丽的爷爷和奶奶(nǎinai)要来中国旅行，他们先坐飞机(fēijī)到广州(Guǎngzhōu)。爸爸和玛丽也去广州，跟爷爷奶奶一起坐火车到北京。

爷爷和奶奶以前来过中国，他们没有到过北京。这一次，玛丽要跟他们去长城(Chángchéng)玩儿，还要去北海、天安门(Tiān'ānmén)，她要给爷爷、奶奶讲很多中国的故事。

LOOK.   SAY.   WRITE

他去公园干什么？

_____。

妈妈去商店买什么？

_____。

_____？

他骑自行车去学校。

_____？

她坐电车上班。

9　打扫教室

打扫 to clean
dǎsao

咱们 we, us
zánmen

窗户 window
chuānghu

开始 to begin, start
kāishǐ

教室 classroom
jiàoshì

擦 to wipe
cā

用 to use
yòng

脏 dirty
zāng

椅子 chair
yǐzi

抹布 rag
mābù

教室里真脏，
The classroom is very dirty.

Jiàoshì li zhēn zāng,

咱们打扫打扫, 好吗?
Shall we give it a cleaning?

zánmen dǎsao dǎsao, hǎo ma?

好。我做什么呢?
Yes. What shall I do?

Hǎo. Wǒ zuò shénme ne?

你擦桌子和椅子。
You wipe the desks and chairs.

Nǐ cā zhuōzi hé yǐzi.

我来擦窗户。
And I will clean the windows.

Wǒ lái cā chuānghu.

我用什么擦桌子呢?
What shall I wipe the desks with?

Wǒ yòng shénme cā zhuōzi ne?

你用抹布。
With a rag.

Nǐ yòng mābù.

看, 那儿有抹布。
Look, there are some rags.

Kàn, nàr yǒu mābù.

咱们开始吧。
Let's begin.

Zánmen kāishǐ ba.

READ ALOUD

今天是星期天,爸爸、妈妈起得很早,他们在打扫屋子呢。哥哥说:"弟弟,快起床! 咱们也打扫打扫吧,屋子太脏了。"弟弟说:"我不,我不,星期天我还想多睡(shuì)一会儿呢!"

哥哥开始打扫了,他用抹布擦窗户、擦桌子和椅子,还擦了地板(dì bǎn floor)。

十点半,弟弟起床了。他看看这儿,看看那儿,屋里真干净(gānjìng clean)。

小猫(māo)看见弟弟,miaomiao叫。小猫在说:"懒,懒,你真懒!"

LOOK. SAY. WRITE

你会写这个汉字吗?

我＿＿＿＿＿。(想)

他用什么吃饭?

＿＿＿＿＿。

27

10 咱们俩谁高

比 than
bǐ

奶奶 grandma,
nǎinai

一点儿 a little
yìdiǎnr

俩 two, both
liǎ

过(来) to come (over)
guò(lai)

胖 fat, chubby
pàng

当然 of course
dāngrán

矮 short
ǎi

还是 or
háishì

28

咱们俩谁高？

Let's see who is taller, you or I?

Zánmen liǎ shuí gāo?

当然我比你高。

Of course I'm taller than you.

Dāngrán wǒ bǐ nǐ gāo.

我比你高

I'm taller than you.

Wǒ bǐ nǐ gāo.

奶奶，您说谁高？

Grandma,
please tell us who is taller?

Nǎinai, nín shuō shuí gāo?

过来，我看看。冬冬比你高。

Come here, let me see.
Dongdong is taller than you.

Guòlai, wǒ kànkan.
Dōngdong bǐ nǐ gāo.

你比冬冬矮一点儿。

You are a little shorter than Dongdong.

Nǐ bǐ Dōngdong ǎi yìdiǎnr.

我胖还是冬冬胖？

Who is more chubby,
Dongdong or I?

Wǒ pàng háishì Dōngdong pàng?

你比冬冬胖。

You are more chubby than Dongdong.

Nǐ bǐ Dōngdong pàng.

READ ALOUD

冬冬大（dà old）还是玛丽大？

　　当然玛丽比冬冬大。

玛丽比冬冬大几岁？

　　玛丽比冬冬大一岁。

今天玛丽忙还是冬冬忙？

　　冬冬比玛丽忙。冬冬今天要赛跑，还要跳高。

LOOK.　SAY.　WRITE

小兔子快还是小乌龟快？

＿＿＿＿比＿＿＿＿。

冬冬早还是芳子早？

＿＿＿＿比＿＿＿＿。

哥哥的屋子脏还是弟弟的屋子脏？

＿＿＿＿比＿＿＿＿。

今天冷还是昨天冷？

＿＿＿＿比＿＿＿＿。

11 下来！下来

干 to do	上 to go up	老鼠 mouse
gàn	shàng	lǎoshǔ
告诉 to tell	出 to go out	后来 later
gàosu	chū	hòulái
事 thing	捉 to catch	可惜 it's a pity
shì	zhuō	kěxī

狄克，下来！下来！
Dick, get down! Get down!

Díkè, xiàlai! xiàlai!

干什么？
Why?

Gàn shénme?

告诉你一件事。
I've got something to tell you.

Gàosu nǐ yíjiàn shì.

你上来吧。
You come up.

Nǐ shànglai ba.

不，你下来吧。快点儿出来！
No, you come down.
Come out at once.

Bù, nǐ xiàlai ba.
Kuàidiǎnr chūlai!

什么事？
What is it?

Shénme shì?

我的小狗捉了一只大老鼠。
My puppy caught a big mouse.

Wǒde xiǎogǒu zhuōle yì
zhī dà lǎoshǔ.

真的吗？
Really?

Zhēnde ma?

后来，老鼠跑了。
But the mouse ran away later.

Hòulái,lǎoshǔ pǎole.

真可惜！
What a pity!

Zhēn kěxī!

兰兰在家吗？

在, 快进来。

兰兰, 你看这个书包好不好？

真好。你昨天去商店了吗？

我昨天去商店了。

你还买什么了？

我还买了两支笔和三张画儿。

LOOK.　SAY.　　WRITE

请_____来!

_____来! 你看这是什么？

你____来, 我告诉你一件事。

你们快____来, 这儿真好。

12　我帮你找哥哥

帮　to help bāng	妹妹 (younger) sister mèimei	让　to let ràng
找　to look for zhǎo	哭　to cry, to weep kū	等　to wait děng
回　to go back huí	还　as well, still hái	

小妹妹，你哭什么？

Why are you crying, little sister?

Xiǎomèimei, nǐ kū shénme?

哥哥去买苹果了，

My brother has gone to get some apples.

Gēge qù mǎi píngguǒ le.

他让我等他，

He asked me to wait for him.

Tā ràng wǒ děng tā,

他还不回来。

But he's still not back.

tā hái bù huílai.

我帮你找哥哥好吗？

I'll help you look for your brother, all right?

Wǒ bāng nǐ zhǎo gēge hǎo ma?

好。

All right.

Hǎo.

看，谁来了？

Look, who's coming.

Kàn, shuí láile?

哥哥，哥哥!

Brother, brother.

Gēge, gēge!

READ ALOUD

今天是儿童节（Értóng jié Children's Day）。冬冬请玛丽、芳子和狄克到他家玩儿。冬冬的爸爸买了四张电影票,请他们去看电影。看什么电影呢？冬冬让他们猜。狄克想了想说:"是《熊猫商店》。"芳子说:"是《小蝌蚪(kēdǒu tadpole)找妈妈》。"冬冬告诉他们,猜的都不对,是《三毛(Sānmáo)的故事》。

LOOK. SAY. WRITE

那儿有一个公园,
咱们____去看看吧。

他们在山上呢,
咱们也____去, 好吗？

咱们快____去吧。

他们呢？
他们都____去了。

36

13 你要买什么

售货员 shop assistant	钱 money	加 plus
shòuhuòyuán	qián	jiā
小朋友 little boy or girl	算 to reckon, to add up	对不起 sorry
xiǎopéngyou	suàn	duì bu qǐ
本子 exercise-book	毛 *mao*	没关系 that's all right, it doesn't matter
běnzi	máo	méi guānxi
多少 how much		
duōshao		

售货员叔叔，您好!
Hello, Uncle (shop assistant)!

Shòuhuòyuán shūshu, nín hǎo!

你好，小朋友。
Hello, little friend.

Nǐ hǎo, xiǎopéngyou.

你要买什么？
Can I help you?

Nǐ yào mǎi shénme?

两个本子，一支笔。
I want two exercise-books and a pencil.

Liǎng ge běnzi, yì zhī bǐ.

好的。
O.K.

Hǎode.

多少钱？
How much is that?

Duōshao qián?

我算算: 三毛加六毛是八毛。
Let me see. Thirty *fen* plus sixty *fen* is eighty *fen*.

Wǒ suànsuan: sān máo jiā liù máo shì bā máo.

不对，不对。我帮你算。
That's not right.
Let me help you.

Bú duì, bú duì.
Wǒ bāng nǐ suàn.

三毛加六毛是九毛。
Thirty *fen* plus sixty *fen* is ninety *fen*.

Sān máo jiā liù máo shì jiǔ máo.

对不起。
I am sorry.

Duì bu qǐ.

没关系。
That's all right.

Méi guānxi.

READ ALOUD

　　妈妈让弟弟买五个面包,两斤(jīn　两斤=1kg)鸡蛋和一斤牛肉。一个面包是一毛五分(fēn　cent)钱,五个面包是七毛五。一斤鸡蛋是一块(kuài　ten *mao*)四毛钱,两斤是两块八。一斤牛肉两块二。请你帮弟弟算算,他今天用了多少钱?
(一块=十毛=一百分,one *yuan* = ten *mao* = one hundred *fen*)

　　七毛五加两块八(毛)是三块五毛五。三块五毛五加两块二(毛)是五块七毛五。对! 他用了五块七毛五。

LOOK.　SAY.　WRITE

对不起!
没关系。

_____。

你要_____?
我要_____。

你要_____?
我要_____。

14 娃娃病了

病 to be ill
bìng

大夫 doctor
dàifu

舒服 well, comfortable
shūfu

疼 ache, pain
téng

咳嗽 to cough
késou

发烧 to have a fever
fāshāo

打针 to have an injection
dǎzhēn

怕 to be afraid
pà

药 medicine
yào

天 day
tiān

娃娃怎么了？
What's the matter with the doll?

Wáwa zěnme le?

大夫，娃娃病了。
Doctor, the doll is ill.

Dàifu, wáwa bìngle.

她哪儿不舒服？
What's wrong with her?

Tā nǎr bù shūfu?

她头疼、咳嗽。
She has a headache and
she is coughing.

Tā tóu téng, késou.

发烧不发烧？
Has she got a fever?

Fāshāo bù fāshāo?

发烧。
Yes, she has.

Fāshāo.

给她打针吧。
Let's give her an injection.

Gěi tā dǎzhēn ba.

不，她怕打针。
No, she's afraid of injections.

Bù, tā pà dǎzhēn.

吃点药，好吗？
Will she take some medicine?

Chī diǎnr yào, hǎo ma?

好。
Yes.

Hǎo.

一天吃三次。
Take it three times a day.

Yì tiān chī sān cì.

READ ALOUD

　　昨天是星期天,冬冬跟小朋友们在外边滑冰。他们玩了半天。

　　冬冬今天没有起床。他头疼、咳嗽,很不舒服。妈妈给他做了面条(miàntiáo),他也不想吃。爸爸请大夫给他看病(kàn bìng examine a patient),大夫说:冬冬感冒(gǎnmào catch cold)了。他给冬冬打针,给他吃药。大夫让冬冬在家里休息(xīuxi rest)两天。

LOOK.　SAY.　WRITE

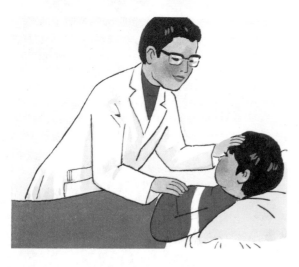
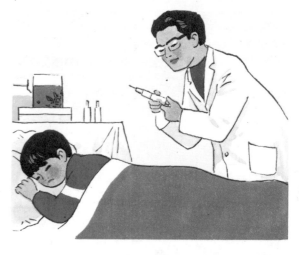

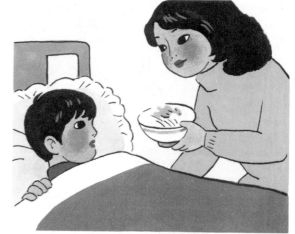

15　找眼镜

眼镜 glasses
yǎnjìngr

放　to put
fàng

忘　to forget
wàng

不用 need not
bú yòng

复习 to review
fùxí

功课 lessons
gōngkè

完 to finish
wán

练习　exercise
liànxí

刚才　just now
gāngcái

啊 oh
ā

奶奶，您在找什么？
Grandma, what are you looking for?

我在找眼镜。
I'm looking for my glasses.

您放在哪儿了？
Where did you leave them?

我忘了。
I've forgotten.

我帮您找。
Let me help you.

不用了，你快去复习功课吧。
There's no need. You must hurry and review your lessons.

我复习完了，也做完练习了。
I've finished reviewing my lessons, and I've done my exercises.

奶奶，您今天用眼镜了吗？
Grandma, did you use your glasses today?

刚才用了。
I used them just now.

您头上是什么？
What's on your head?

啊，找到了。
Oh, we've found them.

Năinai, nín zài zhǎo shénme?

Wǒ zài zhǎo yǎnjìngr.

Nín fàng zài nǎrle?

Wǒ wàngle.

Wǒ bāng nín zhǎo.

Bú yòngle, nǐ kuài qù fùxí gōngkè ba.

Wǒ fùxí wánle, yě zuòwán liànxí le.

Năinai, nín jīntiān yòng yǎnjìngr le ma?

Gāngcái yòngle.

Nín tóu shang shì shénme?

Ā, zhǎodào le.

READ ALOUD

　　玛丽给兰兰打了一个电话, 她要兰兰跟她一起出去玩儿。兰兰正在家里做练习呢。她告诉玛丽, 她很忙, 做完练习还要复习功课, 今天不能出去了。兰兰问玛丽, 昨天开运动会, 丢(diū to lose)的帽子(màozi　hat)找到没有。玛丽说没有, 刚才去商店, 想买一个帽子, 可是(kěshì　but)没有买到。兰兰跟玛丽说, 明天她们一起去商店看看。

LOOK.　SAY.　WRITE

16   把电视打开

把 *preposition showing disposal*
bǎ

电视 (television) TV
diànshì

打 (开) to turn on, to open
dǎ (kāi)

开 to open
kāi

节目 program
jiémù

月亮 the moon
yuèliang

太 too, very
tài

门 door
mén

关 to close
guān

睡觉 to go to bed
shuìjiào

妈妈,我想看电视。
Mum, I want to watch TV.

Māma, wǒ xiǎng kàn diànshì.

你做完算术了吗?
Have you finished your math exercises?

Nǐ zuòwán suànshù le ma?

做完了。
Yes, I have.

Zuòwán le.

今天的汉字你都写对了吗?
Have you copied today's Chinese characters correctly?

Jīntiān de Hànzì nǐ dōu xiěduì le ma?

写对了。
Yes.

Xiěduì le.

好吧,你把电视打开。
All right, turn on the TV then.

Hǎo ba, nǐ bǎ diànshì dǎkāi.

今天有什么节目?
What's the program for today?

Jīntiān yǒu shénme jiémù?

今天有"去月亮上旅行"。
Today there's "A Trip to the Moon".

Jīntiān yǒu "Qù yuèliang shang lǚxíng".

太好了。
That's wonderful!

Tài hǎo lè!

看完了,你把门关上,早点儿睡觉。
Close the door after you have watched TV. Go to bed early.

Kànwán le, nǐ bǎ mén guānshang, zǎo diǎnr shuìjiào.

好。
O.K.

Hǎo.

六点多了,弟弟还在复习功课呢。他想快点儿把功课复习完,七点钟看电视。今天有好节目——足球(zúqiú football)赛。弟弟最喜欢看足球赛。

妈妈进来了。她看见弟弟还在复习,说:"天黑了,快把灯(dēng light)打开!"

七点钟,弟弟把灯关上,把电视打开。

LOOK.　SAY.　WRITE

请你把门_____。

请你把电视机_____。

把窗户_____,好吗?

把收音机(shōuyīnjī)_____,好吗?

17 冬冬的梦

梦 dream
mèng

宇航员 spaceman
yǔhángyuán

飞船 space ship
fēichuán

着 *particle*
zhe (indicating continuous action)

特别 special
tèbié

戴 to wear
dài

帽子 hat
màozi

送 to see sb. off
sòng

嫦娥 fairy Chang'e
Cháng'é

高兴 happy
gāoxìng

轰 boom
hōng

看，那两个宇航员是谁？
Look, who are those two spacemen?

Kàn, nà liǎng ge yǔhángyuán shì shuí?

那是冬冬和玛丽。
That's Dongdong and Mary.

Nà shì Dōngdong hé Mǎlì.

他们坐在飞船里。
They are sitting in a space ship.

Tāmen zuò zài fēichuán li.

他们身上穿着什么呢？
What kind of clothes are they wearing?

Tāmen shēn shang chuānzhe shénme ne?

他们穿着特别的衣服。
They are wearing special clothes.

Tāmen chuānzhe tèbiéde yīfu.

他们头上戴着什么呢？
What kind of hats are they wearing?

Tāmen tóu shang dàizhe shénme ne?

他们戴着特别的帽子。
They are wearing special hats.

Tāmen dàizhe tèbiéde màozi.

飞船把他们送到哪儿去？
Where is the space ship taking them?

Fēichuán bǎ tāmen sòngdào nǎr qù?

飞船把他们送上月亮。
The space ship is carrying them to the moon.

Fēichuán bǎ tāmen sòngshang yuèliang.

他们去月亮上做什么？
What are they going to do on the moon?

Tāmen qù yuèliang shang zuò shénme?

他们去看嫦娥和小白兔。
They want to see Fairy Chang'e and the white rabbit.

Tāmen qù kàn Cháng'é hé xiǎobáitù.

他们真高兴。
They are very happy.

Tāmen zhēn gāoxìng.

十、九、八、七、六、五、四、三、二、一。
Ten, nine, eight, seven, six, five, four, three, two, one.

Shí, jiǔ, bā, qī, liù, wǔ, sì, sān, èr, yī.

轰！ Boom!

Hōng!

READ ALOUD

《去月亮上旅行》是一个很好的电视节目，小朋友们都喜欢看。有两个小宇航员和一只小狗，他们坐着飞船到月亮上旅行。

冬冬特别喜欢这个节目，他也想做一个宇航员。他看完电视，就(jiù then)上床睡觉。他做了一个梦……。

你看，屋子里灯还开着，桌子上放着他的汉字本子。他穿着衣服睡在那儿。

LOOK.   SAY.   WRITE

她穿着什么衣服？

_____。

桌子上放着什么？

_____。

纸上画着什么？

_____。

他戴着什么帽子？

_____。

18 孙悟空飞来了

飞　to fly
fēi

地球　the earth
dìqiú

长城　the Great Wall
Chángchéng

为什么　why
wèi shénme

它　it
tā

因为　because, for
yīnwei

长　long
cháng

所以　so, therefore
suǒyǐ

拿　to hold, to take
ná

桃子　peach
táozi

玛丽, 你看见地球了吗?
Mary, have you seen the earth?

Mǎlì, nǐ kànjian dìqiú le ma?

看见了。地球上是什么?
Yes. What's there on the earth?

Kànjian le. Dìqiú shang shì shénme?

那是中国的长城。
It's the Great Wall in China.

Nà shì Zhōngguó de Chángchéng.

为什么叫它长城?
Why is it called the Great Wall?

Wèi shénme jiào tā Chángchéng?

因为它很长, 所以叫长城。
It's called the Great Wall because it is very long.

Yīnwei tā hěn cháng, suǒyǐ jiào Chángchéng.

冬冬, 你看谁飞来了?
Dongdong, look, who is flying towards us?

Dōngdong, nǐ kàn shuí fēilai le?

啊, 孙悟空飞来了。
Oh, it's the Dear Monkey King.

Ā, Sūn Wùkōng fēilai le.

他手里拿着什么?
What is in his hand?

Tā shǒu li názhe shénme?

他手里拿着一个大桃子。
He is holding a peach.

Tā shǒu li názhe yí ge dà táozi.

孙悟空, 您好!
Hello, Dear Monkey King!

Sūn Wùkōng, nín hǎo!

你也去月亮吗?
Are you going to the moon, too?

Nǐ yě qù yuèliang ma?

是的, 我把桃子送给嫦娥。
Yes, I'm going to give the peach to Chang'e.

Shì de, wǒ bǎ táozi sònggěi Cháng'é.

　　爷爷给冬冬讲过孙悟空和嫦娥的故事。孙悟空是一个猴子(hóuzi monkey)，因为他很勇敢(yǒnggǎn brave)，所以小朋友们都特别喜欢他。孙悟空飞得很快，比飞船还快。他为什么把桃子送给嫦娥呢？因为他自己最喜欢吃桃子。

　　嫦娥是一个仙女(xiānnǚ　fairy)，　她跟小白兔一起住(zhù to live)在月亮上。

LOOK.　SAY.　WRITE

为什么叫它长城？

_____。

冬冬为什么坐飞船？

_____。

他手里拿着什么书？

_____。

她戴着什么手套儿(shǒutàor)？

_____。

19 你长大了做什么

长 to grow
zhǎng
遇 to meet
yù
醒 to wake up
xǐng
被 by
bèi

非洲 Africa
Fēizhōu

森林 forest
sēnlín

猩猩 gorilla
xīngxing

朋友 friend
péngyou

它们 they, them (things, animals)
tāmen

生活 life
shēnghuó

冬冬遇到孙悟空了，后来呢？
Dongdong met the Monkey King, and then?

Dōngdong yùdào Sūn Wùkōng le, hòulái ne?

后来冬冬醒了。
Then Dongdong woke up.

Hòulái Dōngdong xǐngle.

他被奶奶叫醒了。
He was woken up by his grandma.

Tā bèi nǎinai jiàoxǐng le.

啊，他做了一个梦。
Ah, he had a dream.

Ā, tā zuòle yí ge mèng.

冬冬说，他长大了，要做宇航员。
Dongdong says he will be a spaceman when he grows up.

Dōngdong shuō, tā zhǎngdà le, yào zuò yǔhángyuán.

玛丽，你长大了做什么？
What do you want to be when you grow up, Mary?

Mǎlì, nǐ zhǎngdà le zuò shénme?

我长大了去非洲森林。
I want to go to the forests in Africa when I grow up.

Wǒ zhǎngdà le qù Fēizhōu sēnlín.

为什么去非洲森林？
Why do you want to go to the forests in Africa?

Wèishénme qù Fēizhōu sēnlín?

我要跟大猩猩做朋友，
I want to make friends with gorillas,

Wǒ yào gēn dàxīngxing zuò péngyou,

看看它们怎么生活。
and see how they live.

kànkan tāmen zěnme shēnghuó.

芳子呢？
What about Fangzi?

Fāngzǐ ne?

芳子想做一个老师，
Fangzi wants to be a teacher,

Fāngzǐ xiǎng zuò yí ge lǎoshī,

教小朋友《儿童汉语》。
and teach her pupils "Chinese for Children".

jiāo xiǎopéngyou 《ÉRTÓNG HÀNYǓ》.

READ ALOUD

冬冬跟孙悟空一起飞。他们飞得真快,快要到月亮了……真可惜,他被奶奶叫醒了。冬冬说,他长大了要做一个宇航员,坐着飞船到月亮上旅行。兰兰说他长大了要做一个大夫。狄克说他要做一个运动员(yùndòngyuán athlete)。芳子喜欢做老师。她汉语学得很好,她要教很多小朋友学汉语。

小朋友,你长大了做什么呢?你能告诉我吗?

LOOK. SAY. WRITE

奶奶的眼镜被谁找到了?

电视被谁关上了?

伞(sǎn)被兰兰放在哪儿了?

_____。

小乌龟被狄克送给谁了?

_____。

20　新年好

新年 New Year
xīnnián

身体 body
shēntǐ

健康 health, healthy
jiànkāng

快乐 happy, glad
kuàilè

旧 old
jiù

年 year
nián

进步 progress
jìnbù

新 new
xīn

一定 certainly
yídìng

更 more
gèng

老师，新年好！
Happy New Year, teacher!

Lǎoshī, xīnnián hǎo!

阿姨，新年好！
Happy New Year, aunt!

Āyí, xīnnián hǎo!

小朋友，你们好！
Happy New Year, children!

Xiǎopéngyou, nǐmen hǎo!

祝老师和阿姨身体健康，
Good health to our teacher and aunt.

Zhù lǎoshī hé āyí shēntǐ jiànkāng,

生活快乐！
A happy life to you!

shēnghuó kuàilè!

谢谢，孩子们。
Thank you, children.

Xièxie, háizimen.

旧的一年过去了，
The old year is over.

Jiùde yì nián guòqùle,

你们进步很大。
You've made great progress.

nǐmen jìnbù hěn dà.

新的一年开始了，
The new year has started.

Xīnde yì nián kāishǐle,

你们都长了一岁，
You are all a year older.

nǐmen dōu zhǎngle yí suì,

你们的进步一定更大。
You'll certainly make greater progress.

nǐmendè jìnbù yídìng gèng dà.

老师，再见！
Goodbye, teacher!

Lǎoshī, zàijiàn!

小朋友，再见！
Goodbye, children!

Xiǎopéngyou, zàijiàn!

今天是一月一日,冬冬、玛丽、芳子、狄克和兰兰一起到老师家拜年(bài nián pay a new year call)。老师看见他们很高兴,请他们进屋坐。阿姨拿出糖、蛋糕和苹果,让他们吃。

玛丽把贺年片(hèniánpiànr New Year Card)送给老师。她说:"谢谢老师,这一年您辛苦(xīnkǔ work hard)了。"老师说:"你们都是好孩子。你们进步很快,我很高兴。在新的一年里,你们一定学得更好,身体更健康。"

LOOK. SAY. WRITE

祝＿＿＿＿＿！

祝你圣诞(Shèngdàn Christmas)
＿＿＿＿＿！

祝＿＿＿＿＿！

祝＿＿＿＿＿！

VOCABULARY LIST

A

啊　a　oh

矮　ǎi　short

B

把　bǎ　*preposition showing disposal*

吧　ba　*modal particle*

帮　bāng　to help

北海公园　Běihǎi Gōngyuán　Beihai Park

被　bèi　by

本子　běnzi　exercise-book

比　bǐ　to compare, than

病　bìng　to be ill

不用　bú yòng　need not

C

擦　cā　to wipe

猜　cāi　to guess

长　cháng　long

长城　Chángchéng　the Great Wall

嫦娥　Cháng'é　Fairy Chang'e

车　chē　vehicle

出　chū　to go out, come out

船　chuán　boat, ship

窗户　chuānghu　window

次　cì　(*measure word*) time

D

打（电话）　dǎ (diànhuà)　to make (a telephone call)

打（开）　dǎ (kāi)　to turn on, to open

打针　dǎzhēn　to have an injection

大　dà　big, old

打扫　dǎsao　to clean

戴　dài　to wear

61

大夫　dàifu　doctor

蛋糕　dàngāo　cake

当然　dāngrán　of course

到　dào　to go to, to arrive

等　děng　to wait

第　dì

　　ordinal prefix (-st, -nd, -rd)

地球　dìqiú

　　the earth, the globe

电车　diànchē　tram

电话　diànhuà　telephone

电视　diànshì　television, TV

电影　diànyǐng　film

对不起　duìbuqǐ　sorry

多少　duōshao

　　how much, how many

F

发烧　fāshāo

　　to have a fever

放　fàng　to put

放（假）　fàngjià

　　to have (a holiday)

飞　fēi　to fly

飞船　fēichuán　space ship

非洲　Fēizhōu　Africa

复习　fùxí　to review

G

干　gàn　to do

刚才　gāngcái　just now

高　gāo　high

高兴　gāoxìng　happy

告诉　gàosu　to tell

哥哥　gēge　(elder) brother

给　gěi　for, to

跟　gēn　with

更　gèng　more

功课　gōngkè　lessons

故事	gùshi	story		健康	jiànkāng	healthy
关	guān	to close		教室	jiàoshì	classroom
过(来)	guò (lai) to come (here)			讲	jiǎng	to tell
过	guo	*aspectual particle*		节目	jiémù	program

H

				金鱼	jīnyú	goldfish
还	hái	as well, still		进	jìn	to enter
还是	háishì	or		进步	jìnbù	progress
海边	hǎibiān	seaside		旧	jiù	old
轰	hōng	boom				
后来	hòulái	later				
湖	hú	lake				

K

划	huá	to row
回	huí	to return
火车	huǒchē	train

开	kāi	to open
开(会)	kāi (huì) to have (a meeting)	
开始	kāishǐ	to begin, start
咳嗽	késou	to cough

J

可惜	kěxī	it's a pity
家	jiā	home, family
哭	kū	to cry, to weep
加	jiā	plus
快乐	kuàilè	happy, glad
见	jiàn	to see

L

老鼠	lǎoshǔ	mouse
礼物	lǐwù	present
俩	liǎ	two, both
练习	liànxí	exercise
旅行	lǚxíng	to travel

M

抹布	mābù	rag
买	mǎi	to buy
忙	máng	busy
毛	máo	*mao* (1/10 *yuan*, 10 cents)
帽子	màozi	hat
没关系	méi guānxi	that's all right, it doesn't matter
妹妹	mèimei	(younger) sister

门	mén	door
梦	mèng	dream
明天	míngtiān	tomorrow
拿	ná	to hold, to take
奶奶	nǎinai	grandma
能	néng	can
年	nián	year
您	nín	you (polite form singular)

P

爬	pá	to climb
怕	pà	to be afraid
胖	pàng	fat, chubby
跑	pǎo	to run
朋友	péngyou	friend
票	piào	ticket

Q

钱	qián	money
请	qǐng	to ask

R

让	ràng	to let

S

赛跑	sàipǎo	to run a race
森林	sēnlín	forest
山	shān	hill
商店	shāngdiàn	shop
上	shàng	to go up
上班	shàngbānr	to go to work
身体	shēntǐ	health, body
生活	shēnghuó	life
事	shì	thing
售货员	shòuhuòyuán	shop assistant
舒服	shūfu	well, comfortable
暑假	shǔjià	summer holidays, summer vacation
睡觉	shuìjiào	to go to bed
送	sòng	to give (as a present)
送	sòng	to see sb. off
算	suàn	to reckon, to add up
孙悟空	Sūn Wùkōng	the Monkey King
所以	suǒyǐ	so, therefore

T

它	tā	it
它们	tāmen	they, them (things and animals)
太	tài	too, very

糖	táng	sweets, candy	小朋友	xiǎopéngyou	little boy or girl
桃子	táozi	peach	谢谢	xièxie	to thank, thank you
特别	tèbié	special	新	xīn	new
疼	téng	ache, pain	新年	xīnnián	New Year
天	tiān	day	猩猩	xīngxing	gorilla
跳	tiào	to jump	醒	xǐng	to wake up
跳高	tiàogāo	high jump			
听	tīng	to listen			

W

完	wán	to finish
忘	wàng	to forget
喂	wèi	hello
为什么	wèishénme	why
乌龟	wūguī	tortoise

X

下	xià	to get off

Y

呀	ya	*modal particle*
眼镜	yǎnjìngr	glasses, spectacles
要	yào	will, to be going to
药	yào	medicine
爷爷	yéye	grandpa
一定	yídìng	certainly, definite

以前　　yǐqián　　ago, before

椅子　　yǐzi　　chair

一点儿　yìdiǎnr　a little

一起　　yìqǐ　　together

因为　　yīnwei　because, for

用　　　yòng　　to use

宇航员　yǔhángyuán

　　　　　　spaceman

遇　　　yù　　　to meet

月亮　　yuèliang　the moon

运动会　yùndònghuì

　　　　　　sports meet

长　　　zhǎng　　to grow

找　　　zhǎo　　to look for

着　　　zhe　*particle* (indicating

　　　　　　continuous action)

祝　　　zhù　　to wish,

　　　　　　to congratulate

捉　　　zhuō　　to catch

昨天　　zuótiān　yesterday

坐　　　zuò　to sit, to sit down

Z

咱们　　zánmen　　we, us

脏　　　zāng　　dirty

怎么　　zěnme　　how

张　　　zhāng　*measure word*

辅导材料

第一课

1. "请进"、"请坐"是比较客气的用语。

2. "他去哪儿了？""爸爸上班了。""妈妈去商店了。"这些句子最后的语气助词"了"，都表示某个事情或情况肯定已经发生。试比较："他去哪儿？" (Where is he going?)"他去哪儿了？" (Where has he gone?)

第二课

"你跳高了吗？""我没有跳高。"回答"……了吗？"的问题，如果答案是否定的，则在动词前用"没有"（或"没"），句尾去掉语气助词"了"。如"她没跳舞，她唱歌了。""哥哥今天没上班。"

第三课

1. "喂，谁呀？""喂"是打招呼的声音。在打电话或接电话时常用。打电话时通报自己的姓名用"我是……"，询问对方的姓名用"你是……吗？"

2. "你忙不忙？""你能不能来我家？""冬冬来不来？"是将句子谓语中的主要成分（动词或形容词）的肯定形式或否定形式并列起来提问。上述句子的意思跟"你忙吗？""你能来我家吗？""冬冬来吗？"等用"吗"提问是一样的。

注意：动词"有"的肯定形式与否定形式的并列应该是"有没有"。

第四课

"我送你一件礼物。"有一些动词可以带两个宾语。表示"人"的宾语在前，表示"东西"的宾语在后。如"爸爸给我一支笔。""老师教我们算术。"但要注意这种能带两个宾语的动词在汉语中不是很多的。

第五课

1. "您给我们讲个故事，好吗？"介词"给"跟它的宾语"我们"组成介词结构，放在动词前作状语。注意：这个句子不能说成"你讲我们一个故事，好吗？"

2. "这个故事我们听过了。""这个，我们也看过电影了。"助词"过"放在动词后边说明某种动作曾在过去发生，用来强调有过这种经历。如"他以前学过汉语。""我吃过中国菜。"

3. "你们喜欢什么呢？"语气助词"呢"用在疑问句的句尾，使全句的语气缓和。但带"吗"的疑问句后不能再加"呢"。

4. "我们最喜欢听孙悟空的故事。""孙悟空"是中国古典小说《西游记》中的人物，是中国人民喜爱的具有浪漫主义色彩的英雄形象。

第六课

1. "没有去过。""动词＋过"的否定形式是"没（有）……过"。如"他以前没有学过汉语。""我没有吃过中国菜。"

2．"我在那儿划过船。""星期天你跟我们一起去,好吗？"介词"在""跟"等跟它的宾语组成介词结构,放在动词前作状语。"在"的宾语常是表示处所的。"跟"的宾语如果是指人的名词或代词,常与"一起"连用。如"我在学校打电话。""我跟冬冬一起玩儿。"

第七课

1．"不谢。"回答别人感谢的用语。

2．"北海要到了。""我们要下车了。""要＋动词(＋宾语)＋了"表示动作很快就要发生。如"要下雨了。""现在九点了,冬冬要来了。"

3．"您坐这儿吧！"语气助词"吧"用在表示请求、劝告、命令的句子句尾,使整个句子的语气比较缓和。如"我们去吧。""请坐吧。"

第八课

1．"我去海边旅行。""我们坐火车去。"在这两个句子里,主语后边都有两个连用的动词(或动词结构)。后一个动词所代表的动作常常是前一动词所代表的动作的目的("去海边玩儿"),或者前一动词所代表的动作是后一动词所代表的动作的方式("坐火车去")。

2．"这是第一次。"序数的表示法是在数词前加"第"。如"第一""第二""第十二"等。

第九课

1．"咱们"是口语中常用的一个词,它包括谈话的对方;而"我们"则一般不包括谈话的对方。如"我们去北海,你去吗？""咱们一起去,好吗？"

2．"咱们打扫打扫,好吗？"动词重叠使用常表示动作经历的时间短促,或表示轻松、随便,有时也表示尝试。如"我想想。""我听听。""你到我家来玩儿玩儿吧。"

第十课

1．"咱们俩比一比"。"俩"是口语中常用的词。就是"两个"的意思。常说"我们俩","你们俩","他们俩"。"比一比"就是"比比。"单音节动词重叠,中间可以加"一"。如"我想一想。""我听一听。"

2．"我比你高。""你比冬冬矮一点儿。"介词"比"可以用来比较。其词序是:"名词或代词＋比＋另一名词或代词＋形容词"。如"这个教室比那个教室脏。""妈妈比爸爸忙。"

如果要表示比较的结果差别不大时,可以在形容词后用"一点儿"或"点儿"来表示。如"他比我早一点儿。""今天比昨天冷点儿。"

3．"我胖还是冬冬胖？"用连词"还是"连接两种可能的答案,由回答的人来选择,这也是一种提问的方式。如"咱们划船还是爬山？""他是中国人还是日本人？"

第十一课

1．"狄克,下来!下来!""你上来吧。""你快点儿出来。"有些动词后边常用"来"表示动作朝着说话人所在地。如"请进来吧!""他跑来了。""过来,我看看。"

2．"我的小狗捉了一只大老鼠。""了"加在动词后边表示动作的完成。如"他买了三张票。""老爷爷讲了孙悟空的故事。"注意:动词带"了"以后,它的宾语前边一般要带数量词或其它定语。

第十二课

1．"他让我等他。"这类句子前一个动词常带有使令的意义。它的宾语又是后一个动词的主语。如"他请我去他家。""我让他上来。"

2．"咱们进去看看吧。"动词后边加"去"表示动作离开说话人所在地。如"冬冬在山上呢,咱们也上去吧。""玛丽下去了吗?"

第十三课

1．"你好,小朋友。""小朋友"是对儿童的一种称呼。

2．"三毛加六毛是九毛"。中国的人民币的计算单位是"块(kuài)、毛、分(fēn)"。一块等于十毛,一毛等于十分。

3．"对不起"是表示道歉的用语。回答常用"没关系"。

第十四课

"她哪儿不舒服?""她头痛。"在这两个句子里"哪儿不舒服"、"头痛"是谓语,用来说明主语的。而这两个谓语本身又是主谓结构。又如"他汉语很好。""我学习很忙。"

第十五课

"我复习完了。"动词"复习"只表示"review"这个动作。在"复习"后边加补语"完",则表示复习这个动作有了结果(to finish reviewing)。同样,在"找"(to look for)和"找到"(to find),"放"(to put)和"放在"(to put somewhere)以及前面学过的"看"(to look at)和"看见"(to see)等几组词语中,前者都只表示动作,后者则表示动作有了结果。注意:这种句子用"没有"否定。如"没有复习完","没有找到","没有看见"等。

第十六课

1．"你把电视打开。""你把电视关上。"这类带有介词"把"的句子,用来强调说明某些动作对事物的处置及处置的结果。这种句子的词序是:"名词或代词+把+名词或代词(被处置的事物)+动词+其他成分(如动作的结果)"。例如:"请你把门开开。""我要把算术做完。"

2．"写对""打开""关上"也是表示动作有了结果。

第十七课

1．"他们身上穿着什么呢?""他们头上戴着特别的帽子。"动词后加上助词"着",表示动作或动态的持续。如"电视开着吗?""桌上放着本子和笔。"

2."他们要看看嫦娥和小白兔。"嫦娥是中国神话中由人间飞到月亮上的仙女。传说月亮中还有一只玉兔。

第十八课

"因为它很长,所以叫长城。""因为""所以"这两个连词可以同时用在一个句子中,也可以只用其中的一个。如"她病了,所以今天不能到学校。""我帮奶奶找眼镜,因为她眼睛不太好。"

第十九课

"他被奶奶叫醒了。"这类带介词"被"的句子用来表示主语和动词的被动关系。其词序是:"名词或代词(受事)＋被＋名词或代词(施事)＋动词＋其它成分(如动作的结果)"。如"电视被她关上了。""我的书被妈妈找到了。"注意:并不是所有表示被动意思的句子都要用"被"。只有当强调这种被动关系或是要指出施事者时,才用"被"字句。不用"被"也可以表示被动的意思。如"电视关上了。""我的书找到了。"

第二十课

1."新年好"是新年时表示祝贺的用语。

2."你们的进步一定更大。""更"是表示程度的副词,常用在形容词、动词前面表示更高的程度。如"更新""更喜欢""更想"等。

TEACHER'S NOTES

Lesson 1

1. "请进" and "请坐" are expressions of polite request.

2. In sentences like "他去哪儿了？""爸爸上班了。" and "妈妈去商店了。" the modal particle "了" is used to indicate that the event referred to has already taken place. Compare "他去哪儿？" (Where is he going？) with "他去哪儿了？" (Where has he gone？)

Lesson 2

The negative answer to questions with "…了吗？"(e.g. "你跳高了吗？") is made by putting the adverb "没有" (or "没") before the verb and dropping the "了" at the end of the sentence, e.g. "我没有跳高。""他没有跳舞，他唱歌了。""哥哥今天没上班。"

Lesson 3

1. "喂" is used to express an informal greeting, and it is also often used in making or receiving phone calls. In a telephone conversation, "我是…。" is used to tell the other person one's name; while "你是…吗？" or "谁呀？" is used to ask who the other person is.

In "谁呀"，"呀" is a modal particle.

2. Besides quesions with "吗", there are also affirmative-negative questions made by juxtaposing the affirmative and negative forms of the predicative verb or adjective, e.g. "你忙不忙？""你能不能来我家？" (These questions have the same meaning as "你忙吗？""你能来我家吗？")

Notice that affirmative-negative questions with the verb "有" should be "…有没有…".

Lesson 4

Some verbs can take two objects and the object referring to a person precedes the one referring to a thing, e.g. "我送你一件礼物"，"爸爸给我一支笔"，"老师教我们算术". Notice that there are only a small number of verbs in Chinese that can take two objects.

Lesson 5

1. The idea of "Will you please tell us a story？" can not be expressed in a Chinese sentence like "您讲我们一个故事，好吗？" for the verb "讲" can not take two objects. The preposition "给" should be used in this case together with its object "我们" and be placed before

the main verb "讲", i.e. "您给我们讲个故事，好吗？" (Here "给我们" means "for us".)

For the same reason, it is not correct to say "我打电话他了". "我给他打电话了" is the correct form.

2. The aspect particle "过" placed immediately after a verb denotes that some action took place in the past. "过" is often used to express past experience, e.g. "这个故事我们听过了。""这个电影我们也看过了。""我吃过中国菜。"

3. The modal particle "呢" is often added at the end of a question to soften the tone, e.g. "你们喜欢听什么呢？" But it is not used in questions with the particle "吗".

4. "孙悟空" (the Monkey King), a romantic and heroic character in the Chinese mythological novel "Pilgrimage to the West" of 16th century, is well-known and liked by Chinese people.

Lesson 6

1. The negative form of "verb + 过" is "没有 + verb + 过", e.g. "没有去过","他以前没有学过汉语","我没有吃过中国菜".

2. The preposition "在" and "跟" etc. with their objects are often placed before verbs as adverbial modifiers. The object of "在" usually refers to places, e.g. "我在那儿划过船。""我在学校打电话"。 If the object of "跟" is a noun or pronoun referring to a person, it is often used with "一起", e.g. "星期天你跟我们一起去，好吗？""我跟冬冬一起玩儿。"

Lesson 7

1．"不谢" is a reply to "谢谢".

2．The structure "要 + verb (+ object) + 了" indicates that an action is going to take place, e.g. "要下雨了。""现在九点了,冬冬要来了。""北海要到了。""我们要下车了。"

3．The modal particle "吧" can be put at the end of a request, an advice or a command to soften the tone of the sentence, e.g. "您坐这儿吧。""我们去吧。""请坐吧".

Lesson 8

1. If the subject of a sentence is followed by two verbal constructions, the second construction sometimes denotes the purpose of the action expressed by the first one, as in "你去哪儿旅行","我去海边旅行", or the first verb describes the manner of the action expressed by the second, as in "我们坐火车去".

2. The ordinals are formed by putting "第" before the cardinals, e.g. "第一", "第二", "第十二", "第一次".

Lesson 9

1. "咱们" is often used in colloquial speech. It refers to both the speaker and the person spoken to, while "我们" does not include the person spoken to, e.g. "我们去北海,你去吗?""咱们一起去,好吗?"
2. The reduplication of a verb denoting action indicates that the action is of very short duration, and it makes the action sound less rigid or less formal; sometimes it implies that what is done is just for the purpose of trying something out, e.g. "我想想", "我听听", "你到我家来玩儿玩儿吧", "咱们打扫打扫,好吗?".

Lesson 10

1. In "咱们俩比一比", the word "俩" means "两个". It is often used in colloquial speech, e.g. "我们俩", "你们俩", "他们俩".
"比一比" is the same as "比比". The reduplication of the monosyllabic verb can also be formed with "一" inserted in between, e.g. "我想一想", "我听一听".
2. The preposition "比" is used to compare things following this pattern:"noun or pronoun ＋ 比＋ another noun or pronoun+ adjective",e.g. "我比你高" (literally:"I compared to you tall"), "这个教室比那个教室脏", "妈妈比爸爸忙". In "你比冬冬矮一点", "一点" or "点儿" is used after the adjctive to indicate that the difference between the two things is slight, e.g. "他比我早一点儿", "今天比昨天冷点儿".
3. In a choice-type question the two possible choices can be joined by "还是", e.g. "我胖还是冬冬胖?", "咱们划船还是爬山?""他是中国人还是日本人?"

Lesson 11

1. Some verbs are often followed by the directional verb "来" to indicate the action of moving towards the speaker or the thing referred to, e.g. "狄克,下来" (come down),"你上来吧" (come up), "你快点儿出来" (come out), "请进来吧" (come in), "他跑来了" (He is running towards us). "过来,我看看" (come over here).
2. The aspect particle "了" is used after certain verbs to indicate the completion of the action, e.g. "我的小狗捉了一只大老鼠", "他买了三张票", "老爷爷讲了孙悟空的故事". Notice that the object of the verb with the aspect particle "了" is usually modified by a

numeral-measure word or other attributives.

Lesson 12

1. In sentences like "他让我等他", the first verb is often a causative verb such as "请", or "让", and its object is also the subject of the following verb. More examples:"他请我去他家","我让他上来".

2. The directional verb "去" added to some verbs indicates the moving away of the action from the speaker or the thing referred to, e.g. "我送你回去,好吗?""冬冬在上山呢,咱们也上去吧。""玛丽下去了吗?"

3．"三毛" is the name of an orphan boy, a well-known character in the cartoon "The Adventure of Sanmao".

Lesson 13

1．"小朋友" is used as an address to a child, e.g. "你好,小朋友"。

2 The counting units of Renminbi (Chinese currency) are "块 (kuài), 毛,分(fēn)".

One "块" is equal to ten "毛",and one "毛" to ten "分".

3．"对不起" is an expression of apology, meaning "I'm sorry."

The usual reply to it is "没关系".

Lesson 14

In sentences like "她哪儿不舒服?" and "她头痛" the predicates "哪儿不舒服" and "头痛" are formed by subject-predicate-construction. More examples:"他汉语很好","我学习很忙".

Lesson 15

In the sentence "我复习完了", the verb "复习" only indicates the action of "reviewing", but by suffixing the verb "完" the result of "复习" is expressed (to finish reviewing). Similar usages are "找"(to look for) and "找到" (to find), "放" (to put), "放在" (to put on a place) and "看" (to look at) and "看见" (to see). The second verb in each pair of verbs indicates the result of the first verb. Notice that sentences of this type are made negative by placing"没有" before the two verbs, e.g. "我没有复习完","她没有找到眼镜","冬冬没有看见他".

Lesson 16

1. In the sentences "你把电视打开" and "你把电视关上", the preposition "把" is used to emphasize how a thing or person is disposed of and the result, such as the changing of position, the

altering of state, or influence of the action. The structure of this type of sentence is:"noun or pronoun (subject) + 把 + noun or pronoun (disposed of) + verb + other elements (such as the result of the action)".

More examples: "请你把门开开。" "我要把算术作完。"

2．The verbal constructions "写对","打开" and "关上" also express that the action of "写","打" or "关" has achieved its result.

Lesson 17

1．In "他们身上穿着什么呢？" and "他们头上戴着特别的帽子", the particle "着" is added to the verb to indicate the continuation of the action or the state. More examples:"电视开着吗？""桌上放着本子和笔".

2．"嫦娥" is a fairy in a Chinese legend who flew to the moon from the earth. According to the tale, there is also a white rabbit on the moon.

Lesson 18

The conjunctions "因为" and "所以" are either used in a single sentence or seperately, e.g. "因为它很长,所以叫长城。""她病了,所以今天不能到学校。""我帮奶奶找眼镜,因为她眼睛不太好。"

Lesson 19

In the sentence "他被奶奶叫醒了", the preposition"被" is used to express the passive relationship between the subject and the verb. The structure of this type of sentence is:"noun or pronoun (receptor) + 被 + noun or pronoun (performer) + verb + other elements (such as the result of the action)",e.g. "电视被他关了。""我的书被妈妈找到了。"

Notice that not all the passive sentences are constructed with "被". "被" is used only when the passive relationship between the subject and the verb is emphasized, or when the performer of the action is indicated. In Chinese a passive sentence can be formed without "被", e.g. "电视关上了。""我的书找到了。"

Lesson 20

1．"新年好！" is a new year greeting.

2．"更" is an adverb of degree, often used before an adjective or a verb to imply a higher degree, e.g. "祝你们长得更快,进步更大","更新","更喜欢","更想".